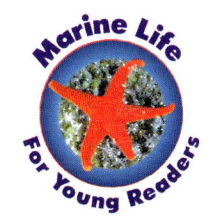

Fish That Hide

Contents

- Many Kinds of Fish   3
- About Fish That Hide   5
- Their Camouflage   7
- Flat Fish   9
- Longnose Hawkfish   11
- Crocodile Fish   13
- Alligator Fish   15
- Lionfish   17
- Frogfish   19
- Starfish Shrimp   23
- Glossary   24
- Index   24

Text by Stanley L. Swartz

Photography by Robert Yin

DOMINIE PRESS
Pearson Learning Group

Many Kinds of Fish

Many kinds of fish live in the ocean. They have different colors, shapes, and **features**.

◀ Diver with Basslet fish

About Fish That Hide

Some fish hide from their enemies. This protects them and keeps them safe. Other fish are **predators**. They hide so they can attack other animals.

◄ Scorpion fish

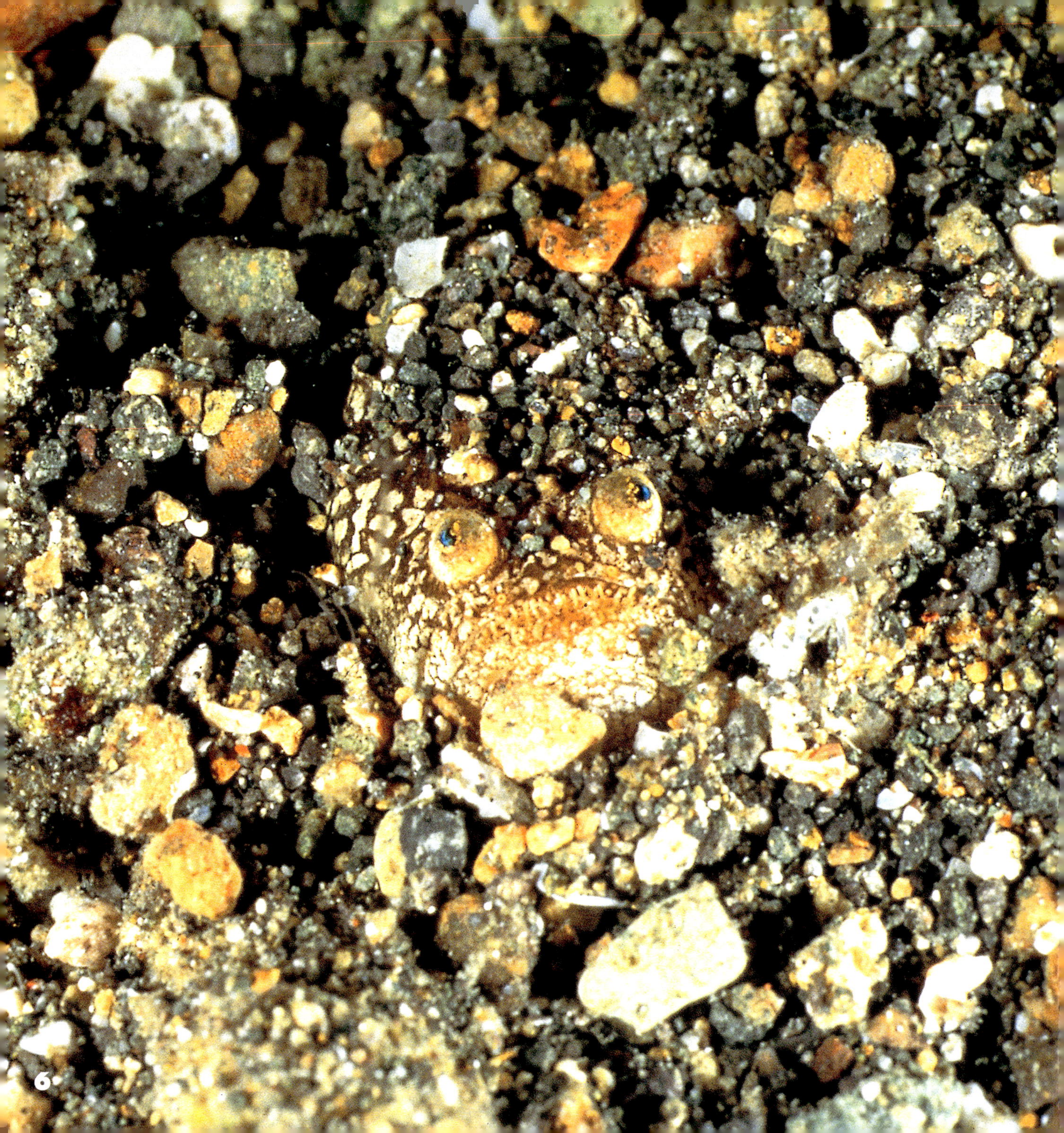

Their Camouflage

Some fish use the way they look to hide from their enemies. This is called **camouflage**.

◀ Stargazer

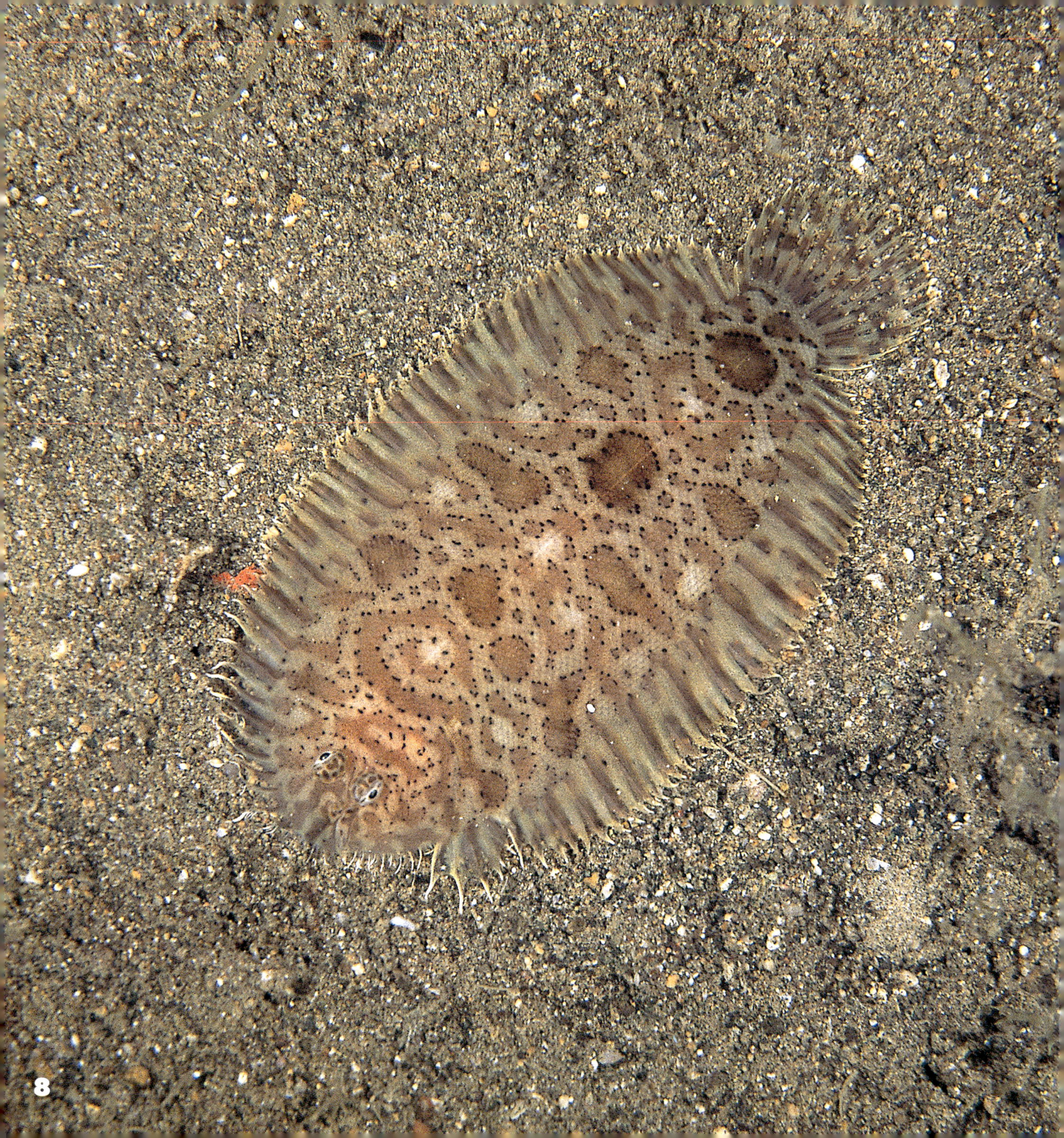

Flat Fish

Flat fish live on ocean bottoms. They have a **flat** body with both eyes on top. Can you see the fish on Page 8?

◀ Flat fish

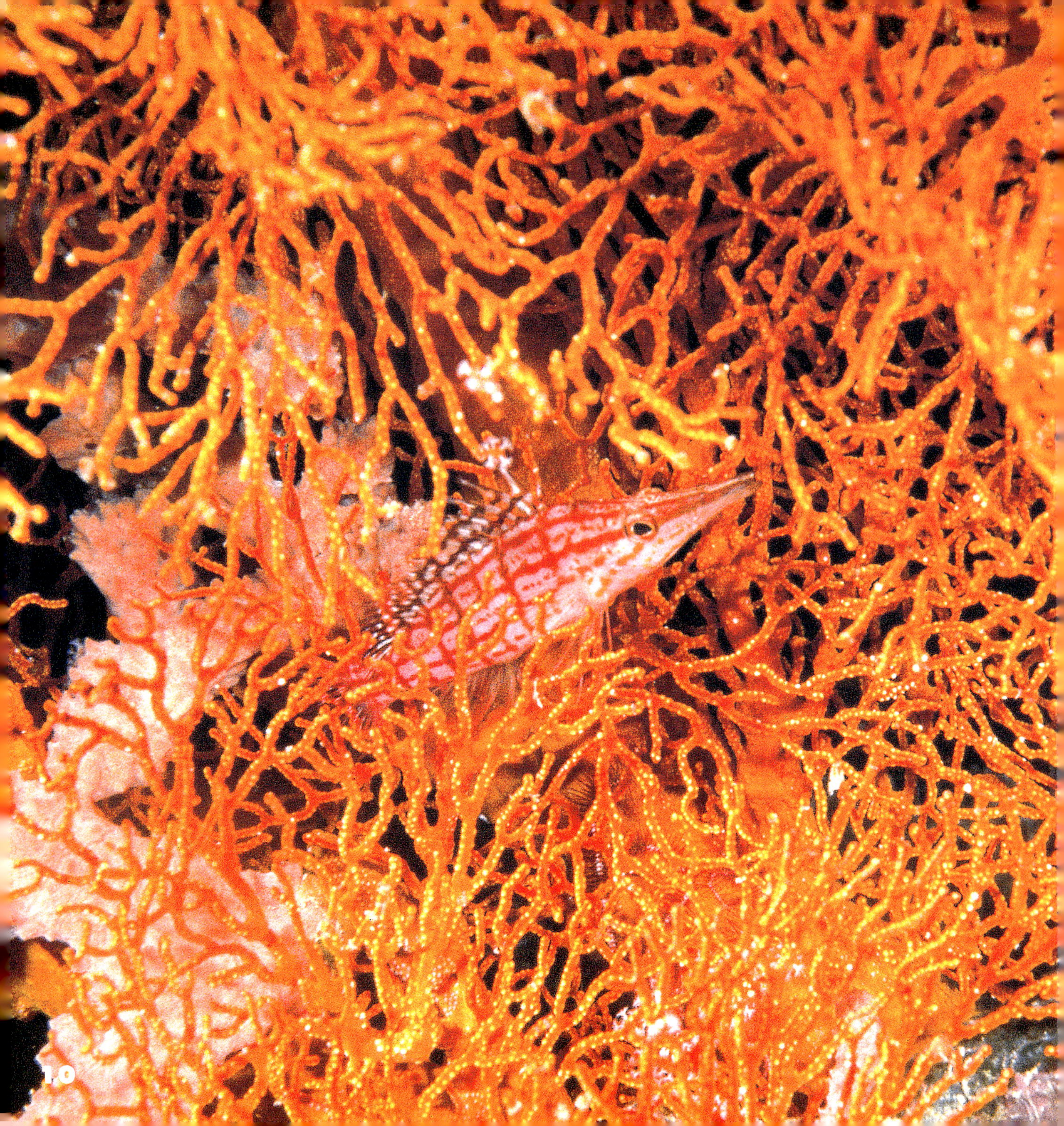

Longnose Hawkfish

Longnose hawkfish live in coral reefs. They like to eat small fish. Their colors change to **match** their surroundings.

◀ Longnose hawkfish

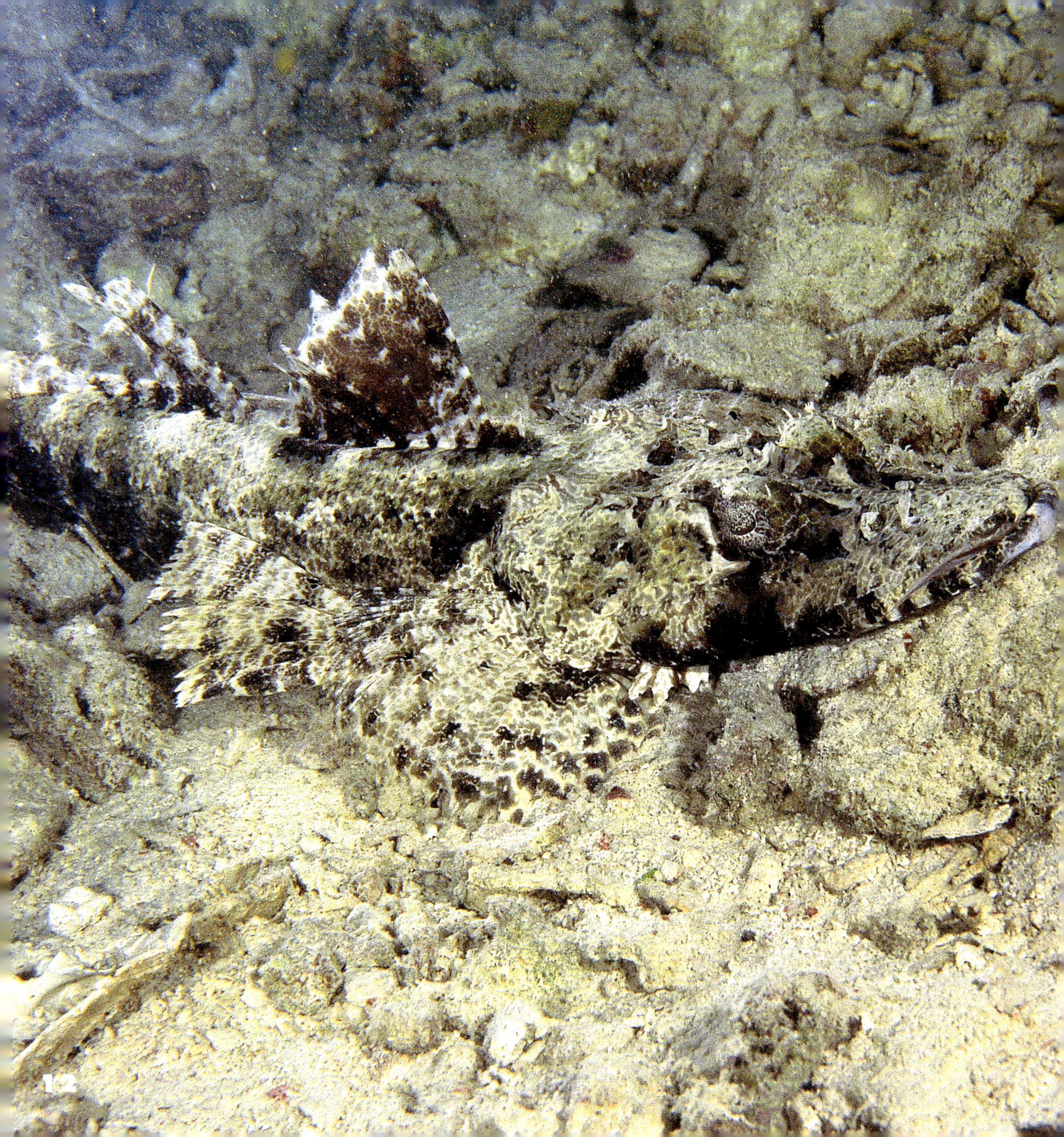

Crocodile Fish

Crocodile fish are predators.

They hide on the ocean's sandy bottom.

Crocodile fish **surprise** their prey.

They can grow to be three feet long.

◄ Crocodile fish

14

Alligator Fish

Alligator fish are **similar** to Crocodile fish. They are much smaller than Crocodile fish. They grow to be six to eight inches long.

◀ Alligator fish

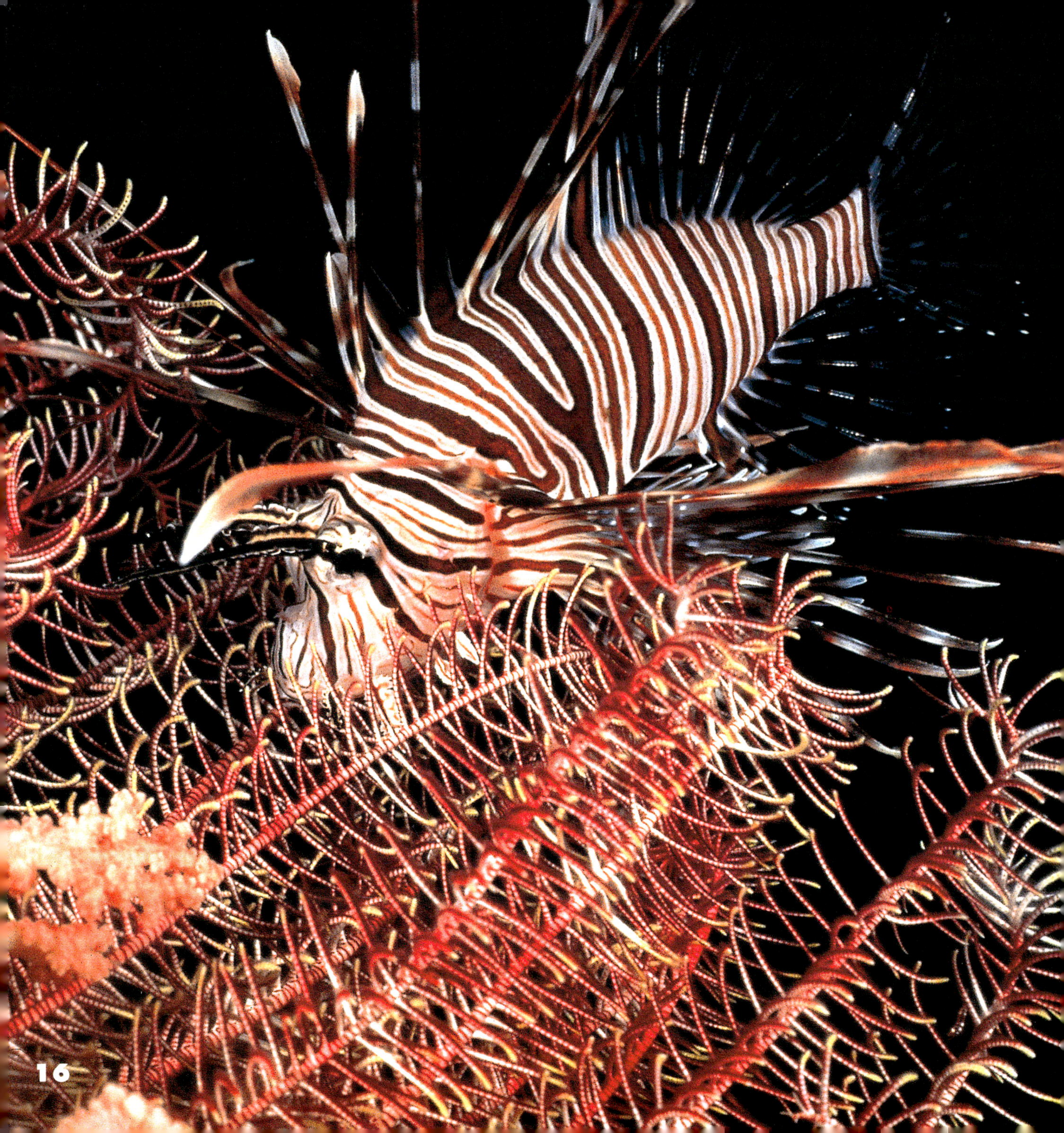

Lionfish

The beautiful colors of the Lionfish blend in with the coral. This makes it hard to see the Lionfish. Its fins have poisonous spines. The fins are used to corner **prey**.

◀ Lionfish

18

Frogfish

Frogfish live in shallow tropical waters. They are among the ugliest fish in the ocean. They are also among the most interesting fish. Frogfish are masters of **disguise**.

◀ Frogfish

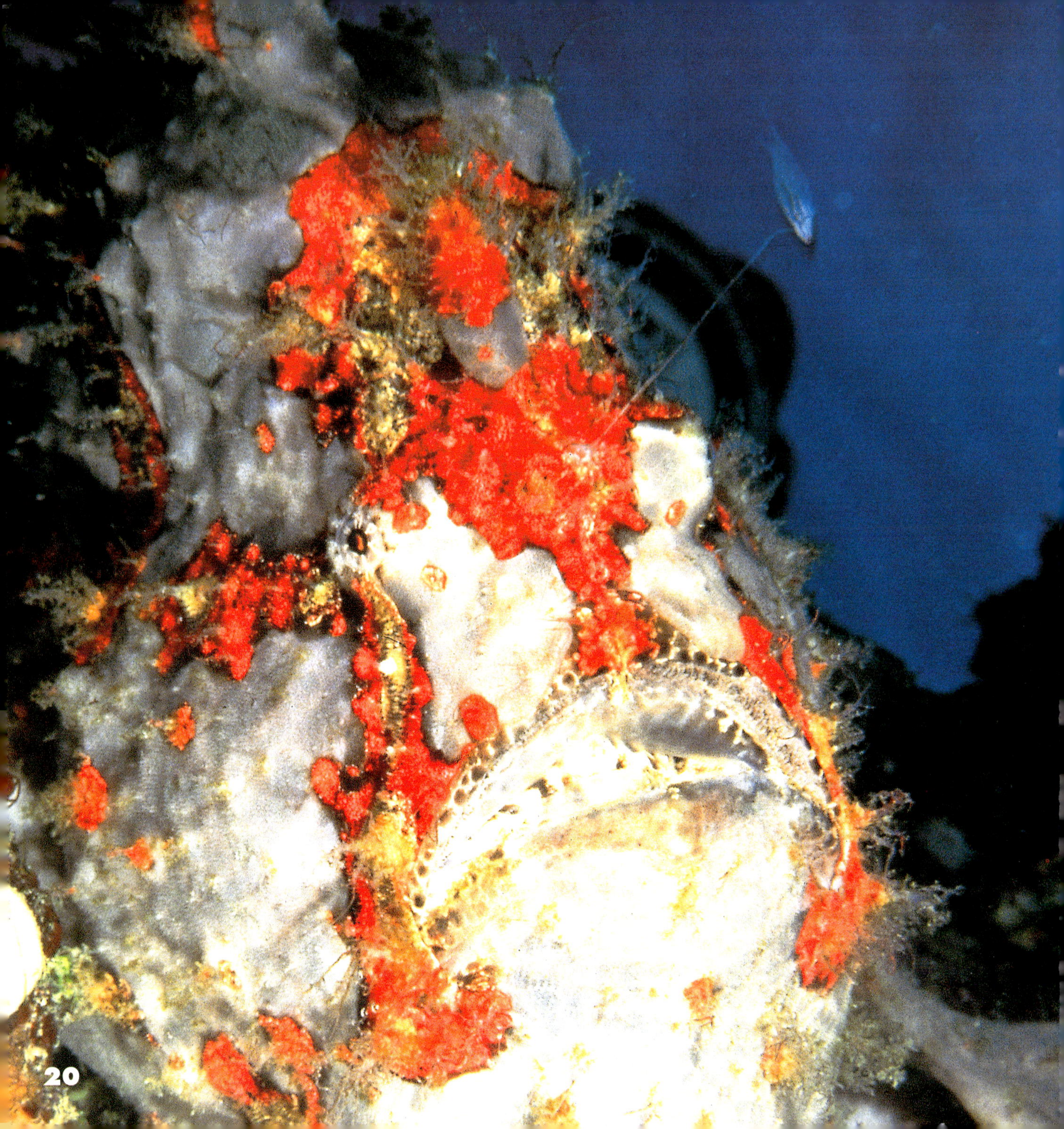

The Frogfish has a fin above its mouth. This fin looks like a worm. Other fish take the **bait**. The Frogfish quickly gobbles its dinner.

◀ Frogfish

Starfish Shrimp

Starfish shrimp live on other sea animals. Many marine animals look like their surroundings. This helps them **survive** in the ocean.

◀ Starfish shrimp

Glossary

bait: Food used to attract and trap an animal
camouflage: To cover or disguise; to hide something
disguise: To conceal your identity
feature: A special or distinct part
flat: An even, or level, surface
match: To be like something
predators: Animals that hunt and kill other animals
prey: An animal that is hunted, caught, and eaten by other animals
similar: To be almost the same
surprise: To come without warning
survive: To stay alive

Index

Alligator fish, 15
bait, 21
camouflage, 7
coral, 17
coral reefs, 11
Crocodile fish, 13, 15
disguise, 19

enemies, 5, 7
eyes, 9
fins, 17
Flat fish, 9
Frogfish, 19, 21
Lionfish, 17
Longnose hawkfish, 11
marine animals, 23

mouth, 21
ocean, 3, 9, 13, 19, 23
predators, 5, 13
prey, 13, 17
spines, 17
Starfish shrimp, 23
tropical waters, 19